THE DEAR FOUR

The Dear Four

Mary Blackwood
Christiane Conésa-Bostock
Karen Knight
Liz McQuilkin

ISBN 978 1 764120 029

Walleah Press
South Launceston
Tasmania, Australia 7249

www.walleahpress.com.au
ralph-walleahpress@proton.me

THE DEAR FOUR

Mary Blackwood

Christiane Conésa-Bostock

Karen Knight

Liz McQuilkin

Dedication

We, the Dear Four, dedicate this collection to the memory of Megan Schaffner who was the fifth member of our poetry group until her death in 2020. Megan always started her emails to us with 'Dear Four'. We remember her with great affection as a dear friend and a very fine poet.

Contents

Mary Blackwood

Meridians

In Sydney
close to midnight
half asleep
I sense the day behind me streaming back
to nine o'clock in Thailand, smoky scents
of grilling fish and lime
the evening woks are firing in Bangkok, and — travel west —
hot darkness falls in Mumbai, fragrant spice
and onions hissing, coconut and cloves
as families are clustering to eat.

Kyiv. The bride and groom
exchanging vows: tuxedo, veil and gauze
the summer light, the broken-window gaze.

In Tuscany, the secateurs away
and gloves hung up against the golden stone
the men take lunch, and doze another hour.

In London, summer crowds for all the bands
at Hyde Park Festival, and shoestring straps
for Billy Joel and Springsteen in the sun.

The world is holding all of us at once.

I fall asleep, tomorrow at my door.
It's dawn in San Francisco, water-clear
and yesterday's mistakes are still not made.

From the Seventeenth Floor

Kuala Lumpur, July 2024

The giant city
pulsing
skeins of light
forever stretches
into steamy dark.

Suitcases to attention.
Dawn alarms.
Tomorrow's stockings
drying in the window.
You check again
your passport
wallet
phone
your boarding pass.

Coming Home

Warm sunrise over Lion Rock
                    the birds:
great egret purple heron ibis dove
the lotus flowers opening to light.

Grey freezing dawn
                    a forest raven caws
                    a possum coughs
snow dusts the creaking trees.

Inside:
            the fire
                    hot tea and toast
                        soft light.

The Transformation

On silver thinning hair the wig sat close,
dark rippled waves held tightly on with pins.
We thought it was her own, until one day
we tiptoed uninvited to her room.

Beside the spectacles, the hearing aid,
the glass for dentures and the spitting cup,
her wig lay on the dressing table, still:
a little brown marsupial at rest.

We backed away in silence, ran outside.
The bits of Grandma guarded her in sleep.

Family Portrait

On Grandma's 96th birthday, June 26th 1959

You know who runs the show, the birthday girl
in oriental jacket, cameo:
her son, his wife, both seventy, behind.
They've given up their sweet retirement years
the sunniest room with views across the bay
the velvet covered chair, the private time.

Three years from now, a fall, a fractured hip
will send her to the bosom of her Lord.
There is no whisper of relief, except
the sense of duty done, with no reward.

Grand-daughter

You skip in front of me to reach the gate.
You're five
completely guileless
unafraid.

I'm old
I wish I didn't know so much
or that the world
was sweeter

or that you
unscathed could skip
between the rocks to come.

Have we always lost our hearts like this?

Did Mary look at Jesus
five years old
and ache to think
of what might lie in store?

Primary Simple Aromas

The sample's in its infancy and hard
to pin to any vintage. All the same
I'll tell you it is linear, needing time
to flesh out and relax
to harmonise and integrate before release.
For now, I'll leave bouquet analysis
as simple as I can:
a hint of ripe strawberry
blue flower
grilled herb
baked brick
blood orange, kirsch and sage....
Complexity can wait another year.

At the Door on Red Shield Day

I'm awfully sorry
but living's expensive
and here's an example
you'll see when I say.
We just got a sofa
powered reclinable
console for storage
headrests adjustable
charging for mobiles
and other devices
cup holders
modular
leather with footrests
it cost us a bomb!

So we'll pass for today.

Rate your experience of this poem

I went to the Kmart on Tuesday.
I bought a new hat for the sun
and leaving, my phone pinged a message
please say how you think we have done.

Did we meet your desire for a sun-hat?
Was the service as good as before?
Give a rating on these six dimensions
and then we can follow up more.

My EasyPark App was sending regards
and pinging excitedly where
in the carpark it asked for my feedback
requesting a rating from there.

At home my computer had missed me, it said
without me the web's not the same
it begged me to rate its performance
for fear I would leave it again.

I wonder if they'll message me
when my time on earth is done
and ask me what I think of how
the funeral was run.

Spinning

The subtle twists of poetry
are threading lively through your hands
you find your creativity
your tapestry precisely hangs.
For just a time it holds your gaze
against the cracked and broken wall.
For just a time the barking world
is silenced by your poetry.

Parallel Worlds

It does not matter who is waging war
or who is voting how, or who has died

the cormorants will line up in the wind
the pelican will stretch black wings to dry
and swallows still will nest below the eaves.

A submarine implodes
a city falls
and violence chases violence round the earth.

The albatross wheels and skims
over the silent sea.

Jetty Pole

Deep in sand
I face the sun and wind
remembering
a hundred years ago:

wood-strong
gale-strong
twenty-four poles strong
shouldering the jetty
hammered in bedrock

the trundle of trolleys
rumble of cartwheels
clatter of sheep hooves
creaking of timber

buffeted
salted
storm-swept and lashed
repaired and then breaking
over and over.

Defeated
the Government
finally left us
me and the others
to rot and to splinter.

The tussocks creep forward.

Nine of us left
standing for ever
grey as the cloud haze
feet on the bedrock
home to the seagulls.

*Constructed in 1911 by the Public Works Department of
Tasmania, the Little Swanport jetty at Lisdillon reached
from the beach out into the bay. It was used to load wool,
salt, wattle bark and the produce of the East Coast. It was
repeatedly damaged by East Coast gales and heavy seas.
Repair efforts were finally abandoned after about ten
years. Only nine weathered poles of the original structure
remain.*

The Good Old Days

As children we would roam the neighbourhood
told only to return at dinnertime.
>*We teased the neighbours' cats up into trees*
>*and lurked near outside toilets to spy.*
We went to bed when asked, we ate our greens
our special treat: a Coke at Christmas time.
>*We crept into each other's rooms at night*
>*to gobble up the lollies pinched that day.*
We learned to read quite young, voraciously,
our favourites, the classics, obviously.
>*We found our uncle's pornographic store*
>*and gasped our way through Peyton Place (the book).*
Our freedom never did us any harm.
>*It taught us how to hide our secret selves.*

If only things were as they used to be
then everyone would turn out well, like me.

Cohorts

At twenty-five
though we were sick with grief
when someone of our age was grabbed away
through rare disease, or suicide, or drugs
we weren't alarmed.
We knew ourselves immortal.

Later we took insurance
didn't smoke.
We started at the gym, and dieted.
This didn't always work.
Sometimes we lost
and cancer stalked, or heart attack, but still
we were a low-risk cohort, middle-aged.

The eighth decade, and conversation turns
to joints (replacement of) and cataracts
dementia, double bypass, and alas
the people who have gone since last we spoke.

They're being called from *our* paddock now.

You Cannot Know

You cannot know which day will be your last
when everything you know will fall away.
The future stopped. The present now the past.

You only know time's travelling so fast
your futile hands would stop the end of day.
You cannot know which day will be your last.

The horses harnessed, chatting slaves, the blast
preserved in ash, an instant in Pompeii.
The future stopped. The present now the past.

It's been the brightest day, the sea like glass.
A wall of water thunders through the bay.
You cannot know which day will be your last.

They called you from the ambulance, aghast.
A game of golf. A normal Saturday …
The future stopped. The present now the past.

The play is written, missing just the cast,
the billboards saying where, and on what day.
You cannot know which day will be your last.
The future stopped. The present now the past.

Christiane Conésa-Bostock

Nativity

Today, the midwife, Madame Tanier
has left behind – hospital smells
strange instruments
and another little brother for us.

My mother believes that for a new soul
to exist, an old one must exit.
As an exchange. One birth, one death.
Her mother is ill in hospital.

Tonight, on icy roads, our father cycles home,
our grandmother's last breath in his back pocket.
Maman swaddled in a pall of mourning
crumbles in his arms. The baby cries.

We are sitting on their bed – no frankincense,
no gold nor myrrh for our mother. Just our silence.
We are hungry too but we don't dare protest.
The logs crackle, as snowflakes waltz past the window.

Downstairs, the crib is almost complete – apart from
baby Jesus – and the Christmas tree decorated.
We think of chocolate, presents and Père Noël
and how we have been robbed of the wonder of Christmas.

The Sewing Machine

My Mother
you were
the maestro
the conductor.

You made the Singer sing
      in harmony
      in cadence
      from adagio
      to allegro
      from marches
      to pastorals.

Your reprises and nocturnes
executed – in a medley –
blouses and shirts
skirts and pants
jackets and coats
even communion dresses.

Silenced
like her ailing artiste
the Singer
was rendered worthless.

Even now, after so many years
I still miss
their joyous chorus
their brisk fugues
their aching hymns
their inexorable finale.

White Library at MONA

An installation by Cuban artist Wilfredo Prieto

It is the mystery of the colour-wheel,
the black missing out of Matisse's découpages.
It is the canvas you ignored yesterday
and might use tomorrow.
It is
Mona Lisa at the Antipodes.

It is the unbroken hymen of a virgin bride
the exchange of caresses and embraces
Sidney Nolan's snake moulting.

It is the smell
of Tutankhamen's open sarcophagi
decomposing mummies
the beauty of Nefertiti
and Cleopatra's nose.

It is the taste of a horse's carcass
and satisfied sex organs.

It is the buzzing of a thousand
dead flies framed into silence,
cascading words written in waterfalls,
video tapes knitted into masks
our armoured sons will wear,
brandishing their swords.

It is
all the cards dealt
the die cast
the verbs you did not conjugate in the present
and the books left unread

where robots with i-pods   will
    imagine
        draw
            write
their future   will
                take photos in white
                        to transform the ordinary
                                into the extraordinary.

Paris 1940s

The Zazous floated through Paris like revolutionary flags.
They jumped in puddles and stayed
in soaked tight puckered pants
which directed the eye of the observer
towards large unpolished shoes.
Salad-oil lustred hair — a little too long —
met soft collars fastened by a woollen tie.
They met their women in existentialist cafés
argued about freedom, Hell and God
under Sartre's Gauloises-fired benevolence.
In the smoky cellars of Saint-Germain des Prés,
young women hid their roll-neck jumpers with fur stoles.
American jazz unleashed striped socks and flat shoes.
Short pleated skirts twirled and swung.

In the métro, the Zazous glared at German occupiers
who, in broken French, chatted up mothers
and at times, with forbidden tenderness,
caressed and startled young faces.
On the streets of Paris, les demoiselles
flouted with arrogance and defiance
their heavy make-up, bright red lipstick
and Pompadour hair-dos,
to provoke the rigid and sombre Nazi officers.

Arrest. Train. Deportation. The road to Hell.
Scissors cut. Razors shaved.
Puddles. Soaked striped pyjamas. Bare feet. Hunger and cold.
Under mocking Aryan gaze, the Revolutionary flags were lowered.

Illuminations

Every year, on the eighth day of December
candle flames, trapped in coloured glasses —
like glow-worms in a damp cave —
dance on the balconies of Lyon.

The golden statue on the basilica of Fourvière —
dedicated to the Virgin Mary
who saved the town from plagues and invasions —
shines like the gilded disc of the moon
above the Rhône embracing the Saône.

In the old quarters of St Jean, all is luminous:
the façades of Renaissance houses
the ancient cathedral, boutiques, restaurants.
The Roman amphitheatres echo Racine and Corneille.

Once, in the hidden corridors of the traboules*
silk-weavers passed and passed again
and on these steps half-eroded by
footsteps, revolutions, wars
I too wander.

Am I an icy revenant?
A distant voyeur revisiting?

Dancing like fireflies
these lights resurrect
my childhood buried
in the sanctuary of memory.

*secret covered passages

A Young Lady holding a Pug Dog

After a painting by François Boucher

Preserved in a frame, alone with her pug dog,
her youth shines – suspended – on canvas.
The painter has captured her timidity.
Her eyes look down in that forlorn place
where a village and memories sleep in silence.

Rouge has already covered the fine skin of her cheeks.
A beauty spot embellishes the corner of her right eye.
Her chaperone prepares the young woman's hair
with grey powder, extensions, pomades and ornaments.

She is not quite ready.

She removes the ribbon from her powdering mantle
and ties it around her pug dog. His ugliness remains unchanged
but she feels for an instant the desire to be chosen.
Her whiteness is strapped tight under a rigid dress.
Matching escarpins and perfume perfect her toilette.

The King pours tea in Madame de Pompadour's boudoir
where a city and memories sleep like a populace.
He awaits the debutantes to be plucked by his lust and desire.

His soft hands untie the stiff bodice dress,
lower the petticoat and caress.
He does not notice her blushing
nor the gentle frisson which invades her body
and heralds her wish to be taken.

She is ready.

Face à Face in an Airport in Paris

It takes great skill
to avoid the other's gaze
when —
to eat a chocolate croissant
and sip a cappuccino—
you take a seat
opposite her
in silence
as if she did not exist
as if she were transparent.

Langue de Boeuf

Hear the bleating of a new-born calf,
its virgin tongue searching for its mother's teat.

Smell the freshly-cut grass on the Lamoura fields
and the dry hay bales stored in the barn.

As small calves become weaners,
witness the passing of each season
in the soaked Jura mountains.

Touch now the coarse surface of the tongue.

Boil it. Scrape the white skin off the pink flesh.

Taste the milk of tender innocence,
the sourness of white vinegar,
and learn from the shepherds of time.

Pieds de Cochon

In his pigsty, farmer laboriously drags pink body.
Unsightly hooves trudge through slush and mud.

At the butcher's shop, they are sold
cleansed, purified and strangely pleasing.

Lady in stilettos totters in.
Buys one for tonight's dinner.

Young man in pig-skin moccasins
procures one, for tomorrow's lunch.

In patent ankle-boots, artist struts in.
With the last two, she will complete her installation.

Pagan Prayer

Our Father, who art in Heaven
give us this day our daily bread
so long   as it is not
                rye
                brown or multigrain
                gluten free
                with soy and lecithin
but a French baguette
light and crusty.

Amen

Dare

Unzip your spine
let me see your bones
from behind
and from the front.

Unzip your lips
and tell me
that you love me.

Dare unzip your heart
tear me in or
tear me out
hear me.

Open your soul
let me see you
as you are
standing
      darling
         unzipped.

Auntie Betty

Auntie Betty, hair in a chignon,
keeps secrets in her bedroom.

On her chest of drawers,
next to an Art Deco woman's bust,
there are garden gloves
a copy of Lady Chatterley's lover
(dog-eared on page 43)
and a bouquet of dried lavender.

She doesn't want me to meet
the man with the dog.
He wears flared pants,
a checked shirt and a straw hat.

I see them kiss
in the garden or in the shed
when uncle Jim is away.

I like looking at their hands promenading,
hers, perfectly manicured,
his, stained with grass and mud.

Once, while they were embracing
he looked up at my window
and waved to me.

Auntie Betty is not the only one to have secrets.
I have a red rose drying
between pages 16 and 17 of my history text book.

Random Objects behind Wardrobes

out of sight of mothers
Playboy magazines with pages
torn by young boys and their fathers

out of sight of husbands
half-finished short stories with artists
lustful letters of a time
when all might have been possible
receipts for expensive perfumes

out of sight of guests
French underwear with holes
woollen socks without partners
intercontinental paper bags
kept for sentimental value

and of course
  dead flies
    decaying moths
      cobwebs and dust.
          Dust…

Taking Flight

After a photograph by Narelle Autio

On a purple sky the bats hang down
tightly wrapped in their capes.
They make music
on the staves of palm branches
which gently bend in the breeze.

They take flight
flapping their outspread digits
and their silk membrane.

Their transparent wings
reflect the moonlight,
capture the warm air
and careless insects.

The photographer gasps,
clicks to seize the sight
and — satisfied —
wraps herself tightly in her cape.

Missing Photograph

I
Fifty years of my life are assembled here
in our garden, between the ivy-covered fence
and the lemon tree laden with fruit.
Thick skin and not much juice.
Like me perhaps.

I waited a long time to steal this rare moment
of togetherness and fix it not only in my memory cells
but in my camera.

And there you stand, looking at me, smiling
my three daughters, two women and one still
a child with a face that borrowed features
from all the others like the final bouquet
of a firework display.
You hold each other tight, fearing to let go.

And you my son now a man
one hand in trouser pocket, the other resting
on a knee poised on a low garden chair,
lost in your thoughts, looking left somewhere
forlorn, a misfit in the canvas of our lives.

II
I am no longer your little boy Mum
the one you dressed in navy blue Cacharel
three-quarter shorts, white shirt, black bow tie
for violin concerts
the one who sang solos, confident and proud.

I am no longer the conductor of the voices
which fill my head, no longer a poet, a troubadour.
I am a man now.
I have seen things you don't want to see:
Rapists, Russian murderers, Nazis and ninjas.
I am a man now of great power if not much means.
I am a psychic who solves crimes
a diplomat to whom Koreans owe peace.
My prayers will heal the sick
and rid earth of evil. I am a man now.

I am no longer your little boy Mum.

III
I watch over you, my maker.

You never took a photograph of me in the humidicrib
and yet there was enough blue light
to warm my tiny body, for you
to witness the nurse's hand flicking me
to jump-start my heart and my lungs.
Enough light to commit to paper
the shape of my head, my hair
the blond soft duvet that covered my skin.

Dad could even have taken a shot of your hand
caressing me but you did not touch me.
Did you? Too little.
Too fragile, too sick.
Too scared to defy the doctor's orders.

You should have fixed on paper
the extent of my fear and my loneliness
my longing for just one kiss, oh my mother.

You should have known better
than to go home and leave me here
to die, cold and alone on my fifth day.

And as I watch you photographing them
I know there is a space on the right-hand side
for me, there, where my brother's eyes are fixing.

Oubliettes*

There is a cloakroom where they keep our lives
in exchange for a three-franc ticket. Every so often
they give us a general anaesthetic
and steal our past.
Memories of yesteryear
and the tentacles of sorrow
seem never to have existed.
They demand we erase
the delirium of pain
and the euphoria of desire.

Today I have paid my dues
and I now know my space.
It has absences that are crosses to bear
stubbed futures and slums of mourning,
skeletons who watch over me
from behind their shutters.
It has bubbles of French Champagne
slumbers in a lover's arms
concertos that make me weep
accordions that make my feet nimble.

Tomorrow I will pay again
and in storage there will be
icy regrets in bleak winter mornings
warm remembrance
in sultry summer evenings

and feelings unbearably present
which will not die
in the lightness of spring
nor the autumn of night.

*From the French 'oublier', to forget, an oubliette is a secret
dungeon where prisoners were forgotten and left to die.*

Karen Knight

So, we've made it to the country

where, in the beginning
we grew carrots and beans
baked bread and biscuits
built chook pens
bred chooks
built more chook pens
laughed with the locals
and
despite the flies
mosquitoes
mouse plagues
and rising damp
we survived somehow.

Lately
the earth seems to be pulling us
towards its rich simplicity.
Our Herculean days
and early nights
are speeding up.

We chase our whispers
around the blackwoods
unaware
of seasons passing.

Shedding Light

I sky-dive through
a funnel of clothes
wipe the dust off
the prehistoric plant

hack a pathway
to the bathroom
with only enough soap
to lather one ear

as the sun lights a match
igniting the river.

With bird seed spreading across
seven continents of floor
early sun turns my hand-reared
goldfinch into that Aztec Gold
never to be seen in colour guides.

Her spits of orchard apple
sprays of millet head
give my kitchen shelves
much more than recipe books.

Her fragrant, liquid song
can be heard over the thrum
of the dishwasher and the croon
of the coffee machine.

Out there,
in the teeth of the wind
my kitten is bringing in
a mouthful of mulberry leaves
through the cat flap.

From what primaeval family
did she steal this gift
as straw was spun into gold
just as the sun was rising?

This morning's newsflash —
two chalky schoolboys
laughing in their language
of sticks and stones
are blinded by the sun
as a lone cyclist
swerves to avoid them.

I'm a tugboat, hauling myself
over the seam-bursting dunes
as the sun spreads itself wide
over a bohemian dawn

and the wind, full of mirth
whistles up my house dress
like a fast balloon.

Stampede

The baby rhinos are coming
in their mother's armoured car.

They're coming fast
muscular and clumsy.

They're coming with heads of steel and husky roars
with bellies full of rhino milk.

They're coming with barbells and boulders
and cumbersome toys.

They're coming with powerful horns
and big baby teeth.

They'll flatten the cat flap
with stout little legs,

crash through the front door
like high-pressure hoses.

The furniture is anchored
throughout the house.

It's a wild day for toddlers
when every cell is rhino cell.

I may need to move
to higher ground.

Painting Florence

I'm closely watching
my newly rescued hen
healing from anaemia
paralysis and possum attack.

She's learning to walk again.
Moonwalking on soft grass.

Each day I give Florence my heart
in different coloured reds
from the paint set I loved as a child –
rose, vermilion, scarlet.

With a smudge of sky
above her head
and a splash of lawn
between her toes

I'm painting my hen back
to life again.

Love Note from Florence

After 'This is Just to Say' by William Carlos Williams

In the red nest box you gave me
I have laid a large brown egg

which you will probably save
for breakfast tomorrow
as it's your birthday.

Trust me
it will be delicious
soft-boiled.

Creamier, eggier
and golden inside.

Goodwill on Garbage Day

It's pick-up day.
The Veolia five-ton truck
with automated arms
has come early.

It's in a hurry —
speeding along dusty Hurdle Road
with garbage-truck music
reverberating around the hills.

I've missed the pick-up:
the pieces of mouldy carpet
balls of rusty wire
and empty bottles of Jacobs Creek bubbly
are still in the day's remains.

One of the men in the truck has spotted me —
noticed I've missed the drop.

They stop at the bridge on their way back
from neighbouring roads, reversing
past the farm gate with yellow duck-crossing sign
past the nearby paddock with a lonely steer.

In brunch coat and cable-knit beanie
I wave my thanks
and they wave back.

Short Life of a Bus

Parked and rusting
in a passed-over graveyard
of vintage automobiles
under the cover
of an atmospheric haze —
the huddled shell
of an REO safety school bus
once life-guard equipped
with no record of tyre blowouts
runs its staggered bell-time
in engine-high grass.

**REO- Ransom Eli Olds (1864-1950), a pioneer
of the American Automobile Industry.*

More than Metal and Rubber

My Hyundai Getz

You await the verdict
as I talk through
your age and illnesses
with an able-bodied mechanic.

I make holy the time
when you taxied
my last worn-out dog
to the vet for that final stretch
to the finishing line.

The serviceman tells me
everything needs replacing
explaining that the dark puddles
in the driveway are not just
incontinent oil leaks.

The grinding brakes
have long lost their footing
and could soon turn you,
my pet machine, into a missile
on wheels.

Do you recall the time
we parked so close
to a fence-line of dairy cows
we could smell the alfalfa
on their breaths?

Before you are towed away
I will spread wild clematis
across your dash — a salute to a life
well lived in the bush, facing the challenges
of unsealed roads together.

Open Day

Chestnut Teal
takes a bullet
in the eye.

Swamp Harrier
falls out of the sky
in shock.

Shelduck
is held and twirled
till its neck breaks.

Black Swan
can't feel the nerves
in its spine.

Grey Teal
has its wings ripped out
by dogs.

Cormorant
flies head on
into the guns.

Pacific Black
hides in the reeds
nostrils above the water.

Recovery

Swift as rabbit calicivirus
gossip has spread:
an intensive-care nurse
has bought the house.

In the past, a young couple
tasted battle on their wedding night.
The bride rabbited on about
the greyish smell in the bedroom.
The honeymoon was brief.

She gave her husband
daily sermons, preaching
that the kitchen was dull
as a grease trap, with no
room to swing a rat.

Her temper rose with the dust
from unsealed roads
and flouted its way through
the cat flap, clouding
all the rooms.

The placid nurse
who comes with fresh air
hygiene and goodwill says
she's going to lift that cloud
and foster the sick, infected
house back to health.

Gratitude

Once in a black moon
we make a blunder:

open the front door
and let a stray dog in.

When one joined a pack
that vandalised our hens

the axe ran blunt
ending their suffering.

We grieved for days, going over
the calamitous event

but we risked it again
and let another dog in.

This is the last one, you said
and I thanked you

as this one came with age
and a deep-seated disease

exhausting our savings
with premium medical care.

Yet, I've never seen a man
love an old dog to the bone
as much as you did.

Quail on the Run

What of the sense of heaviness
when the dead weigh you down
to the rock-ribbed ground
without a blanket for grief?

Do I open a bottle of Dom Perignon
and hope to taste the stars?

Or do I wait for Nature to manifest itself
through a stony beige quail, an escapee
from a hatchery, chip-churring my heart
to restart again?

Quails don't age. Their lives are short-lived.
No grief blankets to comfort them
only white butcher-paper shrouds.

I wish a safe landscape
for this Old World bird
where he can crow
to his captive covey
to join him for a dust bath
in the soft-pillowed earth beneath.

And so this is Christmas

(i)

Before Thanksgiving
before the dispatch
of forty million turkeys
a forty-five pounder called Courage
is given last minute reprieve -
a pardon to live out his life
at a Disneyland Petting Zoo.

(ii)

At a Christmas tree farm
against a backdrop of pines
a family picnics on turkey breast,
corn bread, watermelon, pecan pie.

The parents with handsaw and hatchet
mark their own tree once the children
come down from free wagon rides.

This year, a ten-footer
barely out of its cone
is hacked down and tow-roped
to a lengthy family sedan.

The tree sheds its needles
with strange popping sounds
as its cones snap open.

The car smells like a church.

Advanced Care Directive

When I start coughing
like a Great Dane
and my lungs linger

give me a window
to open and put right
my wrongs.

Read to me hourly:
evergreen
leaf love
moonglade
riverbank
spoondrift
trunk strength.

Feed me enough opioids
to see a blessing of unicorns
in their coltish magic
galloping to greet me.

In the Gloaming

My rescue hen, Florence
is vigilant at this time of day.

Remembering eagles, devils,
quolls and the rogue possum
that almost took her life
she keeps her ear to the ground.

*

Squadrons of wild ducks
have just flown back
to the salty river after
raiding our chicken coops
again.

When it comes to fresh water
and grain, the wild ducks can
storm through any sunset
of the western sky.

*

A moth is tilting its back
to the leadlight lantern

a dusky woodswallow
is singing goodnight.

Angus cows and their calves
are on the slow move back
to their home paddock.

God's rays are sending
shards of colour
from the Old Testament clouds.

*

I am tracing the moon
with my right index finger.

The moon is hard at work
pulling the tides
filling the river

bringing the shorebirds
in large flocks, to gather
and preen at roosting sites.

*

The hens have taken
themselves to bed

their food and water-hoppers
replenished.

The gum trees sleep.
The moon is shining through.

There are flight paths of fire-flies
streaking the sky.

The front porch light is wrapping
an orange glow around me.

Liz McQuilkin

These evenings, our mother retreats
to the laundry to wash or iron,
waiting her turn to use the stove
while able Hiawatha curves his cane.

Ah, the bathroom, Our Father's choice
for calculating, making lists.
Here he sits to plan his trips,
design his huts or boats,
using the only paper close at hand.

As children, we take for granted
that every family lives around The Father.

Thylacine

for my father

In fifty years of hiking
in Tasmania's Central Highlands
he sometimes sensed a presence
a creature watching him

or heard at night
a guttural, coughing bark —
he called it tiger-talk.

With tent flaps open in Summer
he'd savour the Milky Way.
One dawn he woke, aware
of movement encircling him.

A massive, dog-like head
on powerful neck and shoulders
appeared at the opening.

Their eyes locked
a body-length apart.
Time froze, until the creature
backed away, leaving him

shaken
in awe
grateful
for that unexpected visit

and wondering
which of them was more afraid.

Forgotten Time

in The Walls of Jerusalem National Park

Someone has left a watch
encased in marcasite
on a rock by Lake Loretta.

Its oval face is clouded
the winder rusted firm
but case and matching band
glisten in Summer sun.

Imagine a platypus
spying this winking land-fish

a tiger snake prodding the face
with its furious forked tongue

currawongs swooping low
to scrutinise and peck.

Autumn passes. Winter howls.
Watch and rock lie buried deep in snow
as Lake Time grows crystals —
marcasites of ice.

Wilderness Love Song

Come with me into the highlands
far from the frenzy of cities.

Walk with me, traversing slopes
of snow-gum, pandani and pine.

Climb with me, reaching a summit
to look on the roof of the world.

Sing with me, joining the wind
as it flutes across fissures in boulders.

Smile with me, sun-winked and dappled
in forests of autumn-gold fagus.

Laugh with me, paddling in streams
cooling our trek-weary feet.

Lie with me, close in our tent
naming the patterns of stars.

Be with me now and forever
brimful with high-country blessings.

Ode to a Goldfinch called 'Christmas'

for Karen

Little finch, head tilted
you note my presence
a guest in your house:

execute a backward somersault
land neatly near your water bowl
return to your perch for another.

You make sure I'm still watching
not diverted by four galahs outside
sharing breakfast with the hens.

You ring your bell, demand attention
drop to your food bowl, scatter seed
and play with the beads on your abacus.

I really must leave but you draw me back
whistling the opening bars of Beethoven's 5th.
I cannot resist your zest for life.

*

Little finch, you were much smaller
when your human mother found you
early on Christmas Day
severely pecked and bleeding –
the weak one pushed out of the nest.

Twice she put you back.
The third time she took you inside
fed you hourly with a dropper
sang to you, played CDs.
Against the odds you survived.

*

The gods have smiled on you.
Or was it as legend relates:
the One God whose Son you helped
by pecking at the Crown of Thorns
as He carried His Cross to Calvary?

Were you protecting Him
from further pain? Or helping yourself
to thistle seeds? Or both?
That splash of red on your head
a reminder of His Blood?

*

You've been immortalised in paintings
perched on the Madonna's hand.
Your precepts: life is short
we should seize every moment
build goals
take pleasure in small things.

Little finch, you show me
how to live my remaining years.

Out of Sight

My muse is a platypus.
Elusive, he rarely appears
and never when I look for him.

The instant I glimpse him
just as an idea grows, he's gone
submerged in the ripples of my mind.

He teases. Revealing himself
he flaps a flipper in greeting
then disappears into confused currents.

There he is again
flaunting that bizarre form
from duck bill to beaver tail.

Is he a hoax, this cocktail of creatures?
Assembled by some taxidermist genie?
Now he's on his back, looking up

laughing and clambering up a bank
where I can see all of him.
At last, a poem is emerging

but no, he's out of sight
gone to his cave of sedge and sticks
above the water-line

and I must wait
stanzas grounded, words dangling
until he reappears.

Arctic Lover

A Greenland Shark considers his lot.

I am the slow one, searching for a mate.
I cruise and eat and cast an eye about.
I want to settle down, to procreate,
and need to find a wife, wholesome, devout.

I cruise and eat and cast an eye about.
I'd love to court, to fill long winter nights.
I need to find a wife, wholesome, devout,
despite the cold, we'd share such warm delights.

I'd love to court, to fill long winter nights.
I'd smile my hundred teeth, nibble her back.
Despite the cold, we'd share such warm delights
entwining tail-fins, passion well on track.

I'd smile my hundred teeth, nibble her back.
Two centuries old, I still have two to live.
Entwining tail-fins, passion well on track,
I'd be an earnest lover, she'd conceive.

Two centuries old, I still have two to live.
I want to settle down, to procreate.
I'd be an earnest lover, she'd conceive
but I am the slow one, still searching for a mate.

The Greenland Shark can live for more than four-hundred years.
The flesh of this species is toxic and could make nibbling a mate's
back dangerous.

We Cannot Hold a Candle to the French

Written in the style of an Australian bush-ballad

Take the Frenchman, Joseph Pujol, born in 1857.
He was called 'Le Pétomane' which means 'the farting maniac'.
This man had such remarkable abdominal control
he could suck in air per anum then expel it — what a knack.

A baker by profession, he would entertain his clients
by imitating trumpet, flute, bassoon — sounds most refined.
He claimed that he was playing them behind the counter, but
his friends all knew what really lay behind — t'was his behind.

To the Moulin Rouge he took his talent, wooing famous fans:
King Leopold of Belgium, Sigmund Freud, the Prince of Wales.
Le Pétomane would blast the sound effects of cannon fire
and render gentle rectal tones in rhymes of farmyard tales.

The audience cried *ENCORE* when he played 'la Marseillaise'
on an ocarina, through a tube of rubber from his bottom,
but the climax of the evening was his flatulent impression
of the San Francisco Earthquake — ad libbed, ad infinitum.

A true story

Coffin Matters

The showroom exudes a cold detachment.
There's time to ponder the rows, the tiers
of coffins displaying a range of colours,
textures, veneers for every taste:

satin blue or pink interiors,
rosewood, teak or pine exteriors,
no-nonsense handles of practical chrome,
finely wrought wings of sparkling brass.

For me, a cardboard box will do,
or better still a plain white sheet –
a simple shroud is all I need.
And no cremation. Earth not ash.

I'll fertilise my little plot
of carefully chosen, promised land.

Why I admire you, Magnolia liliiflora

You could be having a vibrant July summer
in China, your country of origin.
Here, your branches are bare
while the leaves you dropped in autumn
cover the soil with a mat of mulch.
Now mid-winter, your buds bring promise –
colour to come in my garden –
a glow of maroon and cream.

You are an intimate presence, Magnolia –
sharer of secrets beside my letter-box.
Of modest height, your bearing
is dignified above my cottage clusters
of hellebore, felicia, geranium ....
On frosty mornings, your pale grey boughs
are ghost-like. On bitter nights, a lone street lamp
catches the intricate filigree of your canopy.

I most admire your propensity to bloom.
After that first flush on leafless limbs
you continue, sometimes into December
as petals ease through glossy foliage.
I love the lily-shaped flowers you give
in the spirit of Christmas. No other magnolias
in our street keep their flowers beyond spring.
Once leaves appear, not one blooms – but you.

In a Park by Singapore Harbour

There but for Fortune

go you and I. (Phil Ochs / Joan Baez)

This downpour is so heavy
the tankers in the bay
have disappeared.

We run to a picnic shelter
on its square concrete slab.
In minutes the lawn around it
becomes a lake.

When the thunder retreats
when the rain lightens
the tankers re-emerge
like steely ghosts.

We make a dash
for hotel comfort
past a plastic sheet
strung between two trees.

Beneath, an ancient couple
perch on a makeshift hammock
backs hunched
thin legs dangling

belongings in bags
tied to a rusty bike.

Seeming not to notice
they wait for us to leave
that solitary picnic shelter —
their home.

Sunday Evening on the Right Bank

She's cold, despite her padded jacket.
Face flushed with fatigue,
her heavy frame bears down on swollen feet.

She primed the day at early Mass
before unlocking her stall, displaying
modest trinkets, miniature Eiffel Towers.

In twilight, twelve hours on,
she gathers her goods, wraps them,
stacks them in well-worn cartons,

closes the lid and locks her stall,
the last in a line of green boxes, squatting
like giant frogs along the boulevard.

Last to leave her post,
she shuffles home, alone.
Tomorrow will come too soon.

The Convict Stain

It's 2023. A prisoner's official form
slips from *The Universal Self-Instructor,*
a present to Great-grandmother, Charlotte
from husband, William Hall.

How did Charlotte come by this record?
Why keep it inside this prodigious tome?
Was Convict 4307, Elizabeth Mellor,
perhaps her mother? The document gives details

of birthplace, character, trade and crime.
The Trial in Preston's Court of Petty Sessions.
The Sentence: transportation, seven years
in the penal colony, Van Diemen's Land.

Had Officer Hall discovered his wife's past?
Did he buy the book to teach her
the ways of Tasmania's gentlefolk?
Protect her from stigma: The Convict Stain?

*

1884. Breakfast served and cleared,
Charlotte kisses William goodbye,
stokes the parlour fire, places her book
on the family dining table

and scans the Table of Contents.
Today she'll study Letter Writing,
Household Receipts, Social Etiquette.
But first she unfolds the form:

deciphers the faded longhand, tries to picture
her mother at twenty-one, her own age
but taller: *five foot seven, fair complexion,*
grey eyes, cut above left temple,

a strong, healthy, handsome woman,
factory hand, married, husband and father
at Lancaster .... The words stretch out
in flowing copperplate. Of child, no mention.

Charlotte cannot remember her mother.
Has nothing, not even a keepsake.
Only a convict record she treasures every day
and hides in *The Universal Self-Instructor.*

Moving On

After he'd gone into permanent care
our bed, on his side, squeaked
whenever I moved on mine.

Not a harsh rasping sound
more a sympathetic sigh
gently persistent.

After his death, it stopped
as if the bed at last accepted
that he was gone.

The rest of the house
had already faced his absence
prepared to move on:

a floorboard on the landing
had stopped creaking its loss

the brass front doorstep
shone again

the doorbell, after months of silence
sang out its town-clock chime

and Spring arrived in the garden.

The Art of Dying

I want to find a way to do this well:
not *rage against the dying of the light*
but greet the call to sleep, the tolling bell.

I want to toast the good times and dispel
regrets that shadow moments of delight.
I want to find a way to do this well:

put my affairs in order, say farewell
to doubts, failures, memories that blight
a peaceful ending, sleep, the tolling bell;

mend relationships that faltered, tell
of hurt – given, received – examine, set right
the past, reconcile and do this well;

be joyful, thankful for my life, not dwell
on darkness or anger, sorry for my plight
but listen for the call, the tolling bell.

I search for grace to write this villanelle.
Why not *go gentle into that good night?*
I want to find a way to do this well
and greet the call to sleep, the tolling bell.

The words in italics are taken from Dylan Thomas's
villanelle, 'Do not go gentle into that good night'.

Acknowledgements

Several poems in this collection have appeared in the following publications: *Communion* (2019); *Forty South*, Poets Corner (2023, 2024, 2025); *Net of Hands* (Fellowship of Australian Writers Tasmania Inc, 2009); *Quicksilver Water*, Oasis Women Poets (Walleah Press, 2022)

Christiane Conésa-Bostock won First Prize in the FAW Tasmania Norma and Colin Knight Award in 2021 for her poem, 'Nativity'.

We thank Janet Upcher for her expert editing and proofreading; Adrienne Eberhard and Esther Ottaway for their generous commendations; Jules Witek for photography support with Mary's painting; and Ralph Wessman of Walleah Press, for publishing this manuscript and for his tireless work in supporting Tasmanian writers.

The cover image is the painting 'Another Four' by Mary Blackwood from a photo of Norfolk Bay, Tasmania taken by Jules Witek.

Biographies

Mary Blackwood's poems have been published over four decades since the 1970s. In March 2022, Ginninderra Press published her collected poems under the title *Small Cosmos.* Her rhyming children's picture book *Derek the Dinosaur*, illustrated by Kerry Argent, was first published in 1987 by Omnibus Books, reprinted seven times, and published in America and Korea. Mary worked in Tasmania as a clinical psychologist and later in a number of senior health management roles, most notably in mental health. She retired in 2013. Mary lives in Hobart.

Christiane Conésa-Bostock was born in Lyons, France and has lived in Hobart since the 1970s. Her collection *De passage de France en Tasmanie and other poems* (Picaro Press) was published in 2011 at the same time as the award-winning *Of Things Being Various,* a collaboration with four other poets. She has been published online and in literary reviews in France, Algeria, Australia and the United States. Her latest publication is a bilingual book of poems about the painter Oscar-Claude Monet (Kol Sason Press, 2019). In 2008, the French Government awarded her the Palmes Académiques (rank of Chevalier) for her active contribution to the teaching of French and the diffusion of French culture in Australia.

Karen Knight has been widely published and anthologised since the early 1960s. She has written several poetry collections and chapbooks and was awarded the 2005 Dorothy Hewett Flagship Fellowship Award, the 2007 Arts ACT Alec Bolton Award and the 2011 University of Tasmania Prize (Tasmania Book Awards) for her successful *Postcards from the Asylum* (Pardalote Press, 2008). Karen enjoys collaborations with artists, poets and musicians, and with her photographer husband, Jules Witek, produced *At First Glance: A Tasmanian Landscape in Poetry and Photography* (Forty South, 2022). She and Jules run a mini-sanctuary for rescued creatures on their 'Hurdle Farm' property at Saltwater River, Tasman Peninsula.

Liz McQuilkin, a former English teacher, began writing poetry after retiring. Her collaboration – with Karen Knight, Christiane Conésa-Bostock, Megan Schaffner and Liz Winfield – in the collection *Of Things Being Various* won the FAW National Community Award in 2010 and was published by Forty Degrees South in 2011. Her first solo collection, *The Nonchalant Garden* (Walleah Press), was published in 2014. She collaborated again with Karen Knight in *Renovating Madness: Poems of Willow Court and the Royal Derwent Hospital* (Walleah Press, 2018). Her second solo collection, *Unwrapping Clouds*, was published by Forty South in 2022.

www.ingramcontent.com/pod-product-compliance
Lightning Source LLC
Chambersburg PA
CBHW031256210726
48287CB00003B/1055